German Short Stories for Beginners Book 3

Over 100 Dialogues and Daily Used Phrases to Learn German in Your Car. Have Fun & Grow Your Vocabulary, with Crazy Effective Language Learning Lessons

www.LearnLikeNatives.com

www.LearnLikeNatives.com

© Copyright 2020
By Learn Like A Native

ALL RIGHTS RESERVED

No part of this book may be reproduced, stored in a retrieval system, or transmitted in any form or by any means, without the prior written permission of the publisher.

www.LearnLikeNatives.com

TABLE OF CONTENT

INTRODUCTION	5
CHAPTER 1 The Car / emotions	17
zuversichtlich	30
Translation of the Story	35
The Car	35
CHAPTER 2 Going to A Meeting / telling time	47
Translation of the Story	64
Going to A Meeting	64
CHAPTER 3 Lunch with The Queen / to be, to have + food	75
Translation of the Story	94
Lunch with The Queen	94
CONCLUSION	107
About the Author	113

www.LearnLikeNatives.com

www.LearnLikeNatives.com

INTRODUCTION

Before we dive into some German, I want to congratulate you, whether you're just beginning, continuing, or resuming your language learning journey. Here at Learn Like a Native, we understand the determination it takes to pick up a new language and after reading this book, you'll be another step closer to achieving your language goals.

As a thank you for learning with us, we are giving you free access to our 'Speak Like a Native' eBook. It's packed full of practical advice and insider tips on how to make language learning quick, easy, and most importantly, enjoyable. Head over to LearnLikeNatives.com to access your free guide and peruse our huge selection of language learning resources.

Learning a new language is a bit like cooking—you need several different ingredients and the right technique, but the end result is sure to be delicious. We created this book of short stories for learning German because language is alive. Language is about the senses—hearing, tasting the words on your tongue, and touching another culture up close. Learning a language in a classroom is a fine place to start, but it's not a complete introduction to a language.

In this book, you'll find a language come to life. These short stories are miniature immersions into the German language, at a level that is perfect for beginners. This book is not a lecture on grammar. It's not an endless vocabulary list. This book is the closest you can come to a language immersion without leaving the country. In the stories within, you will see people speaking to each other, going through daily life situations, and using the most common, helpful words and phrases in language.

www.LearnLikeNatives.com

You are holding the key to bringing your German studies to life.

Made for Beginners

We made this book with beginners in mind. You'll find that the language is simple, but not boring. Most of the book is in the present tense, so you will be able to focus on dialogues, root verbs, and understand and find patterns in subject-verb agreement.

This is not "just" a translated book. While reading novels and short stories translated into German is a wonderful thing, beginners (and even novices) often run into difficulty. Literary licenses and complex sentence structure can make reading in your second language truly difficult—not to mention BORING. That's why German Short Stories for Beginners is the perfect book to pick up. The stories are simple, but not infantile. They were not written for children, but the language is simple so that beginners can pick it up.

The Benefits of Learning a Second Language

If you have picked up this book, it's likely that you are already aware of the many benefits of learning a second language. Besides just being fun, knowing more than one language opens up a whole new world to you. You will be able to communicate with a much larger chunk of the world. Opportunities in the workforce will open up, and maybe even your day-to-day work will be improved. Improved communication can also help you expand your business. And from a neurological perspective, learning a second language is like taking your daily vitamins and eating well, for your brain!

www.LearnLikeNatives.com

How To Use The Book

The chapters of this book all follow the same structure:

- A short story with several dialogs
- A summary in German
- A list of important words and phrases and their English translation
- Questions to test your understanding
- Answers to check if you were right
- The English translation of the story to clear every doubt

You may use this book however is comfortable for you, but we have a few recommendations for getting the most out of the experience. Try these tips and if they work for you, you can use them on every chapter throughout the book.

www.LearnLikeNatives.com

1) Start by reading the story all the way through. Don't stop or get hung up on any particular words or phrases. See how much of the plot you can understand in this way. We think you'll get a lot more of it than you may expect, but it is completely normal not to understand everything in the story. You are learning a new language, and that takes time.

2) Read the summary in German. See if it matches what you have understood of the plot.

3) Read the story through again, slower this time. See if you can pick up the meaning of any words or phrases you don't understand by using context clues and the information from the summary.

4) Test yourself! Try to answer the five comprehension questions that come at the end of each story. Write your answers

down, and then check them against the answer key. How did you do? If you didn't get them all, no worries!

5) Look over the vocabulary list that accompanies the chapter. Are any of these the words you did not understand? Did you already know the meaning of some of them from your reading?

6) Now go through the story once more. Pay attention this time to the words and phrases you haven't understand. If you'd like, take the time to look them up to expand your meaning of the story. Every time you read over the story, you'll understand more and more.

7) Move on to the next chapter when you are ready.

www.LearnLikeNatives.com

Read and Listen

The audio version is the best way to experience this book, as you will hear a native German speaker tell you each story. You will become accustomed to their accent as you listen along, a huge plus for when you want to apply your new language skills in the real world.

If this has ignited your language learning passion and you are keen to find out what other resources are available, go to LearnLikeNatives.com, where you can access our vast range of free learning materials. Don't know where to begin? An excellent place to start is our 'Speak Like a Native' free eBook, full of practical advice and insider tips on how to make language learning quick, easy, and most importantly, enjoyable.

www.LearnLikeNatives.com

And remember, small steps add up to great advancements! No moment is better to begin learning than the present.

www.LearnLikeNatives.com

FREE BOOK!

Get the *FREE BOOK* that reveals the secrets path to learn any language fast, and without leaving your country.

Discover:

- The **language 5 golden rules** to master languages at will

- Proven **mind training techniques** to revolutionize your learning

- A complete step-by-step guide to **conquering any language**

www.LearnLikeNatives.com

www.LearnLikeNatives.com

… *www.LearnLikeNatives.com*

CHAPTER 1
The Car / emotions

HANDLUNG

Quentin **interessiert** sich für Autos. Er schaut sich Bilder von Autos an. Er liest jede Nacht die ganze Nacht über Autos. Wenn er sich **langweilt**, stöbert er durch Instagram. Bei den Konten, denen er folgt, dreht sich alles um Autos.

Quentins Freundin ist Rashel. Rashel **amüsiert** sich über Quentins Besessenheit. Autos interessieren sie nicht.

Quentin hat ein Auto. Quentin fährt einen Honda Accord Baujahr 2000. Sein Auto ist grün. Quentin

schämt sich für sein Auto. Er will ein cooles Auto. Er will ein Auto, um mit Rashel durch die Stadt zu fahren. Er träumt von schönen und teuren Autos. Er will ein großes Auto. Kleine Autos findet er langweilig.

In letzter Zeit schaut Quentin ständig auf sein Handy. Wenn Rashel es ansieht, versteckt Quentin das Telefon.

"Quentin, warum versteckst du das Telefon vor mir?" fragt Rashel.

"Nur so", sagt Quentin.

"Das ist nicht wahr!" sagt Rashel.

"Ich verspreche es!" sagt Quentin.

"Dann lass mich den Bildschirm sehen", sagt Rashel.

"Es ist nichts", sagt Quentin. "Vergiss es."

Rashel ist **misstrauisch**, Quentin verheimlicht etwas.

Eines Abends macht Rashel das Abendessen. Quentins Telefon klingelt. Sie kennt die Nummer nicht. Quentin geht ans Telefon.

"Hallo? Oh, ich rufe dich später an", sagt Quentin. Er legt auf.

"Wer ist es?", fragt Rashel.

"Niemand", sagt Quentin.

"Ist es ein Mädchen?" fragt Rashel. Sie ist **eifersüchtig**.

"Nein, ist es nicht", sagt Quentin.

"Wer ist es dann?" fragt Rashel.

"Niemand", sagt Quentin.

"Warum sagst du es mir nicht?" fragt Rashel.

Quentin ist so **wütend**, dass er das Haus verlässt. Er lässt das Essen auf dem Tisch stehen. Es wird kalt. Rashel ist **traurig.** Das Abendessen ist ein Disaster. Rashel ruft ihre Freundin an. Sie reden über das Abendessen. Rashels Freundin denkt, dass Quentin mit einem anderen Mädchen zusammen ist. Rashel ist unsicher. Quentin verheimlicht etwas, sie ist sich sicher.

Quentin sitzt in seinem Auto. Er öffnet seinen Laptop. Er dursucht Anzeigen für Gebrauchtwagen. Es gibt günstige Autos und teure Autos. Er ist **zuversichtlich**. Er sucht ein Auto, das ein ein gutes Geschäft ist. Er hat ein wenig Geld. Er und Rashel sparen Geld. Sie benutzen es für den Urlaub. Dieses Jahr will Quentin ein Auto, keinen Urlaub.

Er sieht eine Anzeige für ein altes Auto. Das Auto ist aus dem Jahr 1990. Das Auto ist ein Jeep. Das Modell ist ein Grand Wagoneer. Er ist **neugierig** auf das Auto. Kein Auto sieht so aus wie dieses Auto. Es hat Holz auf der Außenseite. Quentin findet das cool.

Quentin ruft die Nummer auf der Anzeige an.

"Hallo", sagt ein Mann.

"Hallo", sagt Quentin. "Ich rufe wegen des Autos an."

"Welches Auto?" fragt der Mann.

"Der Jeep", sagt Quentin. "Ich nehme ihn."

"Okay", sagt der Mann.

"Ich hole es morgen", sagt Quentin.

"OK!" sagt der Mann. Er legt auf.

Quentin geht zurück zum Haus. Er fühlt sich **schuldig.** Das Essen ist kalt. Er isst es trotzdem.

Er ist **nervös**. Was wird Rashel über das Auto denken?

Am nächsten Tag holt Quentin das Auto. Quentin liebt das neue Auto. Sein Auto ist ein Jeep Grand Wagoneer von 1990. Es ist ein großes Auto. Es hat Holzpanele an der Seite.

Quention fährt zum Haus. Das Auto hat 120.000 Kilometer. Es ist etwa 30 Jahre alt. Das Auto ist in sehr gutem Zustand. Alles funktioniert. Das Innere ist wie neu. Quentins neues Auto ist etwas Besonderes. Er **schämt** sich nicht das Auto zu fahren. Im Gegenteil, er ist **stolz**, darin durch die Stadt zu fahren. Was gibt es daran nicht zu lieben?

Er klopft an die Tür. Rashel öffnet sie.

"Rashel", sagt er, "Schau!" Quentin zeigt auf das Auto.

"Du hast ein neues Auto?" fragt sie.

"Ja," sagt Quentin. Er lädt Rashel zu einer fahrt ein. Die beiden fahren durch die Stadt. Quentin fährt langsam. Viele Leute starren auf das Auto. Es ist ein besonderes Auto. Einige Männer sehen **neidisch** aus. Sie wollen ein cooles Auto. Quentin ist endlich **glücklich**.

Quentin verbringt jeden Tag mit dem Jeep. Er fährt ihn. Manchmal fährt er einfach nur durch die Stadt. Er liebt das Auto. Er ist **selbstbewusst** im Jeep. Er verbringt jeden Abend damit das Auto zu reinigen. Er poliert die Türen und Fenster jeden Abend. Rashel wartet auf ihn. Er kommt zu spät zum Abendessen. Das macht Rashel **wütend**. Sie hasst den Jeep Wagoneer. Sie glaubt, dass Quentin das Auto mehr liebt als sie. Sie sagt Quentin das und er sagt ihr, sie solle nicht **dumm** sein. Er gibt ihr eine **liebevolle** Umarmung. Er will ihr zeigen, dass sie sich irrt.

www.LearnLikeNatives.com

Am Samstag gehen Rashel und Quentin zum Supermarkt. Quentin fährt sie. Die Fenster sind unten. Quentin trägt eine Sonnenbrille. Er sieht selbstbewusst und von sich selbst überzeugt aus. Er parkt das Auto. Die beiden gehen in den Supermarkt.

Sie kaufen Obst ein.

"Quentin, kannst du vier Äpfel besorgen?" fragt Rashel. Quentin holt die Früchte. Er kommt zurück. Aber er hat vier Orangen.

"Quentin, ich sagte Äpfel!" sagt Rashel.

"Ja, ich weiß", sagt Quentin.

"Das sind Orangen!" sagt Rashel.

"Oh, tut mir leid", sagt Quentin. Er ist **zerstreut**. Er kann sich nicht konzentrieren.

"Was ist los?" fragt Rashel.

"Nichts", sagt Quentin.

"Woran denkst du?" fragt sie.

"Nichts", sagt Quentin. Er hat einen **ängstlichen** Gesichtsausdruck. Er hat einen **besorgten** Blick in seinen Augen.

"Denkst du an das Auto?" fragt Rashel.

"Nein", sagt Quentin.

www.LearnLikeNatives.com

"Doch, das tust du! Ich weiß es! Hol mir ein paar Äpfel", sagt Rashel. Sie ist **entschlossen**, Quentin zur Aufmerksamkeit zu bewegen. Quentin bringt die Äpfel zurück. Er legt sie in den Wagen. Sie beenden den Lebensmitteleinkauf. Quentin ist ruhig. Er wirkt **verschlossen**. Sie gehen zum Auto.

Der Parkplatz ist voll. Quentin inspiziert den Jeep sorgfältig. Er hat **Angst** vor Flecken oder Kratzern. Eine Autotür hinterlässt Spuren, wenn sie gegen eine andere Tür schlägt. Es gibt jetzt viele Autos. Er sieht keine Kratzer. Quentin öffnet das Auto. Er steigt ein.

Rashel bringt die Lebensmittel ins Auto. Sie bringt den Einkaufswagen zurück zum Laden. Sie öffnet die Tür und steigt ein.

"Quentin, ich bin **unglücklich**", sagt sie. Sie weint.

"Was?" sagt Quentin. Er ist **überrascht**. "Was ist los?"

"Dir ist nur das Auto wichtig", sagt Rashel.

"Das ist nicht wahr", sagt Quentin.

"Du hilfst mir bei gar nichts", sagt Rashel.

"Doch! Ich sorge mich um dich", sagt Quentin.

"Wenn du dich um mich sorgst, verkauf das Auto", sagt Rashel.

www.LearnLikeNatives.com

ZUSAMMENFASSUNG

Quentin will ein neues Auto. Er versteckt seine Suche vor seiner Freundin Rashel. Sie fragt ihn, wer anruft. Sie fragt ihn, was er sich ansieht. Aber Quentin hält seine Suche geheim. Quentin findet ein Auto, das ihm gefällt. Er ist endlich glücklich. Er ist jedoch besessen von dem Auto. Rashel wird eifersüchtig. Quentin kann sich nicht im Lebensmittelladen konzentrieren. Er hat Angst, dass jemand das Auto zerkratzt. Quentin hilft Rashel nicht beim Einkaufen. Sie wird wütend. Sie sagt Quentin, dass er sich zwischen ihr und dem Auto entscheiden muss.

VOKABELLISTE

interessiert	interested
gelangweilt	bored
amüsiert	amused
misstrauisch	suspicious

beschämt	embarrassed
eifersüchtig	jealous
wütend	angry
traurig	sad
zuversichtlich	hopeful
neugierig	curious
schuldig	guilty
nervös	nervous
beschämt	ashamed
stolz	proud
neidisch	envious
glücklich	happy
wütend	enraged
dumm	stupid
liebevoll	loving

www.LearnLikeNatives.com

selbstbewusst	confident
zerstreut	distracted
ängstlich	anxious
besorgt	worried
entschlossen	determined
verschlossen	withdrawn
unglücklich	miserable
überrascht	surprised

FRAGEN

1) Was hält Quentin von seinem Auto zu Beginn der Geschichte?

    a) er liebt es

    b) es ihm peinlich ist

    c) es ist zu neu

    d) es ist zu teuer

www.LearnLikeNatives.com

2) Warum wird Rashel beim Abendessen wütend?

    a) sie glaubt, ein Mädchen ruft Quentin an

    b) sie hat Hunger

    c) Quentin verspätet sich

    d) Quentin vergaß, Brot zu kaufen

3) Was macht Quentin im Supermarkt?

    a) er zahlt für alles

    b) er bringt Orangen statt Äpfeln

    c) er verschüttet Milch

    d) er achtet auf Rashel

4) Was hält Quentin von seinem neuen Auto?

    a) es ist zu neu

    b) es ist zu klein

    c) er ist stolz darauf

d) es ist ihm peinlich

5) Was machen Quentin und Rashel am Ende der Geschichte?

    a) sich küssen

    b) sich nach dem Streit versöhnen

    c) das Geschäft verlassen

    d) einen Streit haben

ANTWORTEN

1) Was hält Quentin von seinem Auto zu Beginn der Geschichte?

    b) es ist ihm peinlich

2) Warum wird Rashel beim Abendessen wütend?

    a) sie glaubt, ein Mädchen ruft Quentin an

3) Was macht Quentin im Supermarkt?

    b) er bringt Orangen statt Äpfeln

4) Was hält Quentin von seinem neuen Auto?

    c) er ist stolz darauf

5) Am Ende der Geschichte, Quentin und Rashel:

    d) einen Streit haben

www.LearnLikeNatives.com

Translation of the Story

The Car

STORY

Quentin is **interested** in cars. He looks at pictures of cars. He reads about cars all night, every night. When he is **bored**, he scrolls through Instagram. The accounts he follows are all about cars.

Quentin's girlfriend is Rashel. Rashel is **amused** by Quentin's obsession. Cars do not interest her.

Quentin has a car. Quentin drives a 2000 Honda Accord. His car is green. Quentin feels **embarrassed** by his car. He wants a cool car. He wants a car to drive around town with Rashel. He dreams of nice cars, expensive cars. He wants a big car. Small cars are boring.

Lately, Quentin looks at his phone all the time. When Rashel looks at it, Quentin hides the phone.

"Quentin, why do you hide the phone from me?" asks Rashel.

"No reason," says Quentin.

"That's not true!" says Rashel.

"I promise it is!" says Quentin.

"Then let me see the screen," says Rashel.

"It's nothing," says Quentin. "Forget about it."

Rashel is **suspicious**. Quentin is hiding something.

One night, Rashel makes dinner. Quentin's phone rings. She does not know the number. Quentin answers the phone.

"Hello? Oh. I will call you later," says Quentin. He hangs up.

"Who is it?" says Rashel.

"Nobody," says Quentin.

"Is it a girl?" asks Rashel. She is **jealous**.

"No it is not," says Quentin.

"Then who is it?" asks Rashel.

"Nobody," says Quentin.

"Why won't you tell me?" asks Rashel.

He is so **angry**; Quentin walks out of the house. He leaves the food on the table. It gets cold. Rashel is **sad**. The dinner is a waste. Rashel calls her friend. They talk about the dinner. Rashel's friend thinks Quentin is with another girl. Rashel is unsure. Quentin is hiding something. She is sure.

Quentin sits in his car. He opens his laptop. He searches adverts for second-hand cars. There are cheap cars and expensive cars. He is **hopeful**. He looks for a car that is a good bargain. He has a little money. He and Rashel save money. They use it for vacation. This year, Quentin wants a car, not a vacation.

He sees an advert about an old car. The car is from the year 1990. The car is a Jeep. The model is a Grand Wagoneer. He is **curious** about the car. No cars look like this car. It has wood on the outside. Quentin thinks that is cool.

Quentin calls the number on the advert.

"Hello," says a man.

"Hello," says Quentin. "I am calling about the car."

"Which car?" asks the man.

"The Jeep," says Quentin. "I'll take it."

"Ok," says the man.

"I'll come get it tomorrow," says Quentin.

"Ok!" says the man. He hangs up the phone.

Quentin goes back to the house. He feels **guilty**. Dinner is cold. He eats it anyway. He is **nervous**. What will Rashel think about the car?

The next day, Quentin gets the car. Quentin loves the new car. His car is a 1990 Jeep Grand Wagoneer. It is a big car. It has wood panels along the side.

Quentin drives to the house. The car has 120,000 kilometers. It is about 30 years old. The car is in very good condition. Everything works. The interior is like new. Quentin's new car is special. He does not feel **ashamed** driving. On the contrary, he feels **proud** driving through town. What is not to love?

He knocks on the door. Rashel opens it.

"Rashel," he says. "Look!" Quentin points at the car.

"You have a new car?" she asks.

"Yes," says Quentin. He invites Rashel to ride. The two drive around town. Quentin drives slow. Many people stare at the car. It is a special car.

Several men look **envious**. They want a cool car. Quentin is finally **happy**.

Quentin spends every day with the Jeep. He drives it. Sometimes he has nowhere to go. He just drives around town. He loves the car. He feels **confident** in the Jeep. He spends every evening cleaning the car. He polishes the doors and windows every night. Rashel waits for him. He is late for dinner. This makes Rashel **enraged**. She hates the Jeep Wagoneer. She thinks Quentin loves the car more than he loves her. She tells Quentin this and he tells her not to be **stupid**. He gives her a **loving** hug. He wants to show her she is wrong.

On Saturday, Rashel and Quentin go to the supermarket. Quentin drives them. The windows are down. Quentin wears sunglasses. He looks **confident** and sure of himself. He parks the car. The two go into the supermarket.

They shop for fruit.

"Quentin, can you get four apples?" asks Rashel. Quentin goes to get the fruit. He returns. But he has four oranges.

"Quentin, I said apples!" says Rashel.

"Yeah, I know," says Quentin.

"These are oranges!" says Rashel.

"Oh, sorry," says Quentin. He is **distracted**. He cannot concentrate.

"What is wrong?" asks Rashel.

"Nothing," says Quentin.

"What are you thinking about?" she asks.

"Nothing," says Quentin. He has an **anxious** look. He has a **worried** look in his eyes.

"Are you thinking about the car?" asks Rashel.

"No," says Quentin.

"Yes you are! I know it! Go get me some apples," says Rashel. She is **determined** to make Quentin pay attention. Quentin brings back the apples. He puts them in the cart. They finish grocery shopping. Quentin is quiet. He seems **withdrawn**. They go to the car.

www.LearnLikeNatives.com

The parking lot is full. Quentin inspects the Jeep carefully. He is **afraid** of marks or scratches. A car door leaves marks when it hits another door. There are many cars now. He does not see any scratches. Quentin unlocks the car. He gets in.

Rashel puts the groceries in the car. She returns the cart to the store. She opens the door and gets in.

"Quentin, I am **miserable**," she says. She is crying.

"What?" says Quentin. He is **surprised**. What is wrong?

"You only care about the car," says Rashel.

"That's not true," says Quentin.

"You don't help me do anything," says Rashel.

"I do! I care about you," says Quentin.

"If you care about me, sell this car," says Rashel.

www.LearnLikeNatives.com

CHAPTER 2
Going to A Meeting / telling time

HANDLUNG

Thomas verlässt sein Wohnhaus. Es ist ein schöner Tag, die Sonne scheint, die Luft ist frisch. Thomas hat heute eine wichtige Besprechung. Thomas ist Geschäftsführer eines Unternehmens. Heute trifft er sich mit neuen Investoren. Er ist auf das Treffen vorbereitet und fühlt sich entspannt.

Es ist **acht Uhr morgens**. Thomas geht die Straße entlang. Er ist extra zu früh um mehr **Zeit** zu haben. Er will nicht zu spät kommen. Er möchte keinen Stress haben.

www.LearnLikeNatives.com

Thomas lebt in einer Großstadt. Es gibt überall große Gebäude. Taxis fahren vorbei. Viele Autos fahren vorbei. Thomas geht gerne zu Fuß. Manchmal nimmt er die U-Bahn.

Thomas will frühstücken. Er hält an einem Café. Das Café ist gemütlich. Musik spielt im Café. Thomas will eine Backware.

"Was möchten Sie?" fragt der Barista.

"Einen Muffin bitte", sagt Thomas.

"Blaubeere oder Schokolade?" fragt der Barista.

"Blaubeere, bitte", sagt Thomas.

"Etwas zu trinken?" fragt der Barista.

"Einen Kaffee", sagt Thomas.

"Schwarz?" fragt der Barista.

"Nein, mit etwas Sahne", sagt er.

"Zum mitnehmen?" fragt der Barista. Thomas schaut auf seine Uhr. Es ist **acht Uhr dreißig**. Er hat Zeit.

"Für hier" sagt Thomas. Er setzt sich und isst. Er sieht Menschen vorbeigehen. Thomas schaut wieder auf seine Uhr. Es ist neun Uhr **auf die Minute**. Er steht auf. Thomas wirft den Müll weg und geht auf die Toilette. Er nimmt seine Uhr ab, um seine Hände zu waschen. Seine Uhr ist aus Gold und er mag es nicht, sie nass zu machen. Sein Telefon klingelt.

"Hallo", sagt Thomas.

"Sind Sie im Büro?" fragt Thomas' Sekretärin.

"Noch nicht", sagt Thomas. "Ich bin auf dem Weg."

Er verlässt das Café. Thomas geht in Richtung U-Bahn. Er hat Zeit, also braucht er kein Taxi. Er schaut wieder auf seine Uhr. Aber seine Uhr ist nicht da. Thomas hat Panik. Er denkt über den Morgen nach. Hat er sie zu Hause gelassen? Nein. Er erinnert sich, dass er die Uhr abnimmt und sich die Hände wäscht. Die Uhr ist im Café.

Thomas rennt zurück zum Café.

"Verzeihung", sagt er zum Barista.

www.LearnLikeNatives.com

"Haben Sie eine goldene Uhr?", fragt er.

"Nur eine **Sekunde**", sagt der Barista. Er fragt seine Kollegen. Niemand hat die Uhr.

"Nein," sagt der Barista. Thomas geht auf die Toilette. Er schaut am Waschbecken nach. Die Uhr ist nicht da. Jemand hat die Uhr, denkt Thomas. Er hat keine Zeit mehr um weiter zu suchen.

"Verzeihung", sagt er wieder zum Barista.

"Wie spät ist es?" fragt er.

"Zehn Uhr und 9 Minuten", sagt der Barista.

"Danke," sagt Thomas. Thomas eilt. Er hat die Besprechung um Viertel vor elf. Er eilt zur U-Bahn-Station. Es gibt eine lange Schlange, um Tickets zu kaufen. Er wartet fünf **Minuten**.

"Wissen Sie, wie spät es ist?" fragt Thomas eine Frau.

"Es ist zehn Uhr **dreißig**", sagt sie. Thomas ist spät dran. Er verlässt die lange Schlange. Er geht auf die Straße. Er ruft ein Taxi. Alle Taxis sind besetzt. Schließlich hält ein Taxi. Thomas steigt ins Taxi.

"Wo möchten Sie hin?" fragt der Fahrer.

"Zur 116. und Park", sagt Thomas.

"Okay", sagt der Fahrer.

"Bitte beeilen Sie sich", sagt Thomas. "Ich muss **pünktlich** zu einem Meeting."

"Ja, mein Herr", sagt der Fahrer.

Thomas trifft am Büro an. Er rennt aus dem Taxi und die Treppe hoch. Seine Sekretärin grüßt ihn. Thomas ist verschwitzt!

"Die Besprechung ist **in einer Stunde**", sagt die Sekretärin. Thomas wischt sich den Schweiß aus dem Gesicht.

"Gut", sagt Thomas. Er bereitet sich auf das Treffen vor. Sein Hemd ist verschwitzt. Es riecht schlecht. Thomas beschließt, ein neues Hemd für das Treffen zu kaufen.

Thomas geht zum Laden die Straße runter.

"Hallo, der Herr", sagt die Verkäuferin, "wie können wir Ihnen helfen?"

"Ich brauche ein neues Hemd", sagt Thomas. Die Verkäuferin nimmt Thomas mit, um ihm die Hemden zu zeigen. Es gibt rosa Hemden, braune Hemden, Hemden mit Karomustern und Hemden mit Schottenmustern. Die Verkäuferin redet viel. Thomas ist nervös wegen der Zeit.

"**Wie spät ist es?**" fragt Thomas die Verkäuferin.

"Es ist **fast Mittag**", sagt die Verkäuferin.

"Okay", sagt Thomas. "Geben Sie mir das braune Hemd." Die Verkäuferin bringt das braune Hemd zur Kasse. Sie faltet das Hemd. Sie **lässt sich Zeit**.

www.LearnLikeNatives.com

Thomas' Handy klingelt, es ist seine Frau.

"Schatz, wir essen um 19 Uhr zu **Abend**", sagt sie.

"Okay, Liebes", sagt Thomas. "Ich kann jetzt nicht wirklich reden."

"Okay", sagt sie. "Ich will nur nicht, dass du um neun Uhr **abends** nach Hause kommst."

"Keine Sorge", sagt Thomas.

"Tschüss", sagt seine Frau. Thomas legt auf.

"Entschuldigen Sie", sagt Thomas. "Ich habe es eilig. Ich brauche das Hemd nicht eingepackt."

"Okay", sagt sie. Thomas zahlt und verlässt den Laden. Er wechselt sein Hemd, während er die Straße entlang geht. Leute starren, er eilt ins Büro.

"Es **wird auch Zeit**", sagt seine Sekretärin, als er hereinkommt. Sie warten auf das Treffen. Die Investoren sitzen am Tisch. Thomas grüßt sie.

"Ich mag dein Hemd, Thomas", sagt einer der Investoren.

"Danke", sagt Thomas. "Es ist neu." Thomas legt sein Telefon ab und schaltet seinen Computer ein.

"Danke, dass Sie gekommen sind", sagt Thomas. "Ich habe eine Präsentation, die etwa 15 Minuten lang ist."

Thomas fragt seine Sekretärin: "Wie spät ist es?"

www.LearnLikeNatives.com

"Es ist **zwölf Uhr fünfzehn**", sagt sie.

"Danke", sagt Thomas. "Meine Uhr ist weg."

"Warum schauen Sie nicht auf Ihr Telefon, wenn Sie wissen möchten wie spät es ist?", sagt einer der Investoren.

"Natürlich", sagt Thomas. Er ist so an seine Uhr gewöhnt, dass er vergisst, dass er das Telefon für die Uhrzeit nutzen kann!

"Ich muss der letzte Mensch auf der Welt sein, der nur eine Uhr benutzt um die **Uhrzeit zu erfahren**", sagt Thomas. Alle lachen.

ZUSAMMENFASSUNG

Thomas beginnt seinen Tag mit viel Zeit. Er frühstückt und entspannt. Er geht ins Bad und lässt seine Uhr im Bad. Als er es bemerkt, geht er zurück zum Café. Die Uhr ist weg. Jetzt muss er jeden fragen, wie spät es ist. Er kommt zu spät ins Büro. Glücklicherweise wird sein Treffen um eine Stunde verschoben. Er geht, um ein neues Hemd zu kaufen. Das dauert länger, als er erwartet. Er eilt zu dem Treffen. Als er wieder nach der Zeit fragt, wird ihm klar, dass er auf sein Telefon schauen kann um die Uhrzeit zu erfahren. Das Treffen beginnt.

VOKABELLISTE

Es ist ___ Uhr	It is ___ o'clock
morgens	in the morning
Zeit	time
halb ___	half past ___
auf die Minute	on the dot
zweiter	second

www.LearnLikeNatives.com

Wie spät ist es?	What time is it?
____ und ____	____ oh ____
Vormittags	a.m.
Viertel vor ____	quarter to ____
Minuten	minutes
Wie spät ist es?	Do you have the time?
____ dreißig	____ thirty
pünktlich	on time
in einer Stunde	in an hour
Wie spät ist es?	What's the time?
fast	nearly
Mittag	noon
lässt sich Zeit	takes her time
Nachmittags	p.m.
abends	at night

wird auch Zeit	about time
____ Minuten lang	____ minutes long
____ fünfzehn	____ fifteen
Uhrzeit erfahren	tell the time

FRAGEN

1) Warum verliert Thomas seine Uhr?

   a) sie fällt ab

   b) er lässt einen Fremden sie halten

   c) er macht eine Wette

   d) Er nimmt sie ab, um sich die Hände zu waschen

2) Wo wohnt Thomas?

   a) in einer Kleinstadt

b) in einer Stadt mit wenig Verkehrsmitteln

c) in einer Großstadt

d) auf dem Land

3) Thomas hat Glück, weil:

a) er hat nette Kollegen

b) seine Sitzung verschoben wird

c) die U-Bahn ist nicht voll

d) er seine Uhr nicht verliert

4) Thomas sagt der Verkäuferin, das Hemd nicht einzuwickeln, weil:

a) er zu spät kommt zu seiner Besprechung

b) der Schweiß auf seinem Hemd sichtbar ist

c) seine Frau am Telefon wartet

d) er es hasst Tüten zu verschwenden

5) Am Ende der Geschichte lacht jeder, weil:

    a) Thomas' Hemd verschwitzt ist

    b) Thomas verlegen ist

    c) Thomas vergisst, dass man die Uhrzeit auf dem Telefon ablesen kann

    d) Thomas seine Uhr verliert

ANTWORTEN

1) Warum verliert Thomas seine Uhr?

    d) Er nimmt sie ab, um sich die Hände zu waschen

2) Wo wohnt Thomas?

c) in einer Großstadt

3) Thomas hat Glück, weil:

    b) seine Sitzung verschoben wird

4) Thomas sagt der Verkäuferin, das Hemd nicht einzuwickeln, weil:

    a) er zu spät kommt zu seiner Besprechung

5) Am Ende der Geschichte lacht jeder, weil:

    c) Thomas vergisst, dass man die Uhrzeit auf dem Telefon ablesen kann

Translation of the Story

Going to A Meeting

STORY

Thomas leaves his apartment building. It is a beautiful day. The sun shines. The air is fresh. Thomas has an important meeting today. Thomas is the CEO of a company. Today he meets with new investors. He is prepared for the meeting. He feels relaxed.

It is **eight o'clock in the morning**. Thomas walks down the city street. He is early. He wants extra **time**. He does not want to be late. He does not want to stress.

Thomas lives in a big city. There are tall buildings everywhere. Taxis drive by. Lots of cars drive by.

Thomas likes to walk. Sometimes he takes the subway.

Thomas wants to eat breakfast. He stops at a café. The café is relaxed. Music plays. Thomas wants a baked good.

"What would you like?" asks the barista.

"A muffin please," says Thomas.

"Blueberry or chocolate?" asks the barista.

"Blueberry, please," says Thomas.

"Anything to drink?" asks the barista.

"A coffee," says Thomas.

"Black?" asks the barista.

"No, with a bit of cream," he says.

"To go?" asks the barista. Thomas looks at his watch. It is **half past eight.** He has time.

"For here," says Thomas. He sits down and eats. He watches people walk by. Thomas looks at his watch again. It is nine o'clock **on the dot**. He gets up. Thomas throws out the trash and goes to the bathroom. He takes off his watch to wash his hands. His watch is gold and he doesn't like to get it wet. His phone rings.

"Hello," says Thomas.

"Sir, are you at the office?" asks Thomas's secretary.

"Not yet," says Thomas. "I'm on my way."

He leaves the coffee shop. Thomas walks towards the subway. He has time, so he doesn't need a taxi. He looks at his watch again. But his watch is not there. Thomas feels panic. He thinks back over the morning. Did he leave it at home? No. He remembers taking off the watch and washing his hands. The watch is at the coffee shop.

Thomas runs back to the coffee shop.

"Excuse me," he says to the barista.

"Do you have a gold watch?" he asks.

"Just a **second**," says the barista. He asks his colleagues. No one has the watch.

"No," says the barista. Thomas goes to the bathroom. He looks by the sink. The watch is not there. Someone has the watch, Thomas thinks. He has no time to look any more.

"Excuse me," he says to the barista again.

"**What time is it?**" he asks.

"**Ten oh nine a.m.**" says the barista.

"Thanks," says Thomas. Thomas hurries. He has the meeting at a quarter to eleven. He rushes to the subway stop. There is a long line to buy tickets. He waits for five **minutes**.

"Do you have the time?" Thomas asks a woman.

"It's ten **thirty**," she says. Thomas is late. He leave the long line. He goes to the street. He waves for a taxi. All the taxis are full. Finally, a taxi stops. Thomas gets into the taxi.

"Where are you going?" asks the driver.

"To 116th and Park," says Thomas.

"Ok," says the driver.

"Please hurry," says Thomas. "I need to be **on time** for a meeting."

"Yes, sir," says the driver.

Thomas arrives to the office. He runs out of the taxi and up the stairs. His secretary says hello. Thomas is sweaty!

"Sir, the meeting is now **in an hour**," says the secretary. Thomas wipes the sweat off his face.

"Good," says Thomas. He prepares for the meeting. His shirt is sweaty. It smells bad. Thomas decides to buy a new shirt for the meeting.

Thomas goes to the store down the street.

"Hi, sir," says the salesperson. "How can we help you?"

"I need a new dress shirt," says Thomas. The salesperson takes Thomas to see the shirts. There are pink shirts, brown shirts, checked shirts, and plaid shirts. The salesperson talks a lot. Thomas is nervous about the time.

"**What's the time?**" Thomas asks the salesperson.

"It's **nearly noon**," says the salesperson.

"Ok," says Thomas. "Give me the brown shirt." The salesperson takes the brown shirt to the cash register. She folds the shirt. She **takes her time**.

Thomas's phone rings. It is his wife.

"Honey, we have dinner at seven **p.m.**," she says.

"Ok, dear," says Thomas. "I can't really talk right now."

"Ok," she says. "I just don't want you to come home at nine o'clock **at night**."

"Don't worry," says Thomas.

"Bye," says his wife. Thomas hangs up the phone.

"Excuse me," says Thomas. "I'm in a hurry. I don't need the shirt wrapped."

"Ok," she says. Thomas pays and leaves the store. He changes his shirt as he walks down the street. People stare. He hurries to the office.

"It's **about time**," says his secretary when he walks in. They are waiting in the meeting. The investors sit around the table. Thomas says hello.

"I like your shirt, Thomas," says one of the investors.

"Thanks," says Thomas. "It is new." Thomas sets his phone down and turns on his computer.

"Thank you for coming," says Thomas. "I have a presentation. It is about fifteen minutes long."

Thomas turns to his secretary. "What time is it?"

"It is **twelve fifteen**," she says.

"Thanks," says Thomas. "My watch is missing."

"Why don't you look at your phone for the time?" says one of the investors.

"Of course," says Thomas. He is so accustomed to his watch that he forgets he can look at the phone for the time!

"I must be the last person in the world to only use a watch to **tell the time**," says Thomas. Everyone laughs.

www.LearnLikeNatives.com

CHAPTER 3
Lunch with The Queen / to be, to have + food

HANDLUNG

U rsula **ist** ein junges Mädchen. Sie lebt in London, England. Sie geht zur Schule. Sie liebt es zu backen. Sie **hat** eine Leidenschaft: die königliche Familie. Sie will eine Prinzessin **sein**.

Eines Abends ist Ursula zu Hause. Ihre Mutter bereitet das Abendessen zu. Sie **haben** etwas Neues. Ihre Mutter bringt die Teller zum Tisch.

"Was **sind** das?" fragt Ursula.

"Das sind Lauche", sagt Ursulas Mutter.

"Oh, ich mag keinen Lauch", sagt Ursula.

"Probier sie", sagt ihre Mutter. Sie probiert sie. Sie übergibt sich fast.

"Ich **bin** krank", sagt Ursula.

"Nein, bist du nicht", sagt ihre Mutter.

"Bitte, gib mir anderes **Gemüse**", sagt Ursula. "**Karotten**, **Brokkoli**, **Salat**?"

"Ach, Ursula, dann iss nur dein **Fleisch**", sagt ihre Mutter. Sie macht den Fernseher an. Sie schauen die Nachrichten. Der Bericht handelt von der Königin von England. Ursula hört auf zu essen. Sie gibt gut acht.

"Königin Elisabeth regiert England seit 68 Jahren", heißt es im Nachrichtenbericht. "Sie ist mit Prinz Phillip verheiratet, sie haben vier Kinder."

Die Nachrichten berichten über die Königin. Sie lebt im Buckingham Palace. Sie ist sehr gesund, trotz ihres Alters.

"Ich will den Buckingham Palace besuchen", sagt Ursula.

"Ja, Liebes", sagt ihre Mutter. Sie schauen sich die Sendung an. Das Programm kündigt einen besonderen Wettbewerb an. Eine Person kann einen Besuch im Buckingham Palace gewinnen.

Der Sieger isst mit der Königin zu **Mittag**. Ursula schreit.

"Ich **muss** gewinnen!" schreit sie.

"Ich bin mir nicht sicher", sagt ihre Mutter. "Viele Leute nehmen am Wettbewerb teil."

Ursula schaut sich die Sendung an. Sie lernt einzutreten. Sie fotografiert sich selbst beim Essen. Dann postet sie es in den sozialen Medien. Sie sieht sich die Sendung an, in dem es um das Essen mit der Königin geht. Sie sieht zu, wie sie zeigen, was einem Prinzen aus dem Südpazifik, beim Essen mit der Königin, zugestoßen ist.

Die Königin ist auf einem Boot mit dem Prinzen. Sie servieren **Nachtisch**. Der Prinz vergisst, die Königin zu beachten. Er nimmt ein paar

www.LearnLikeNatives.com

Trauben und **Kirschen** von den **Früchten** auf dem Tisch und legt sie in seine Schüssel. Er schüttet Sahne über sie. Er streut **Zucker** darüber. Er fängt an zu essen, und dann merkt er, dass die Königin nicht angefangen hat zu essen. Er macht einen großen Fehler. Die Königin nimmt ihren Löffel. Sie isst ein Stück. Das beruhigt den Prinzen. Es ist ihm sehr peinlich.

"Es gibt Regeln, um mit der Königin zu essen?" fragt sie ihre Mutter.

"Natürlich", sagt ihre Mutter.

"Was zum Beispiel?" fragt Ursula.

"Nun, die Königin beginnt das **Essen** und beendet das Essen", sagt Ursulas Mutter.

"Du meinst, du kannst erst essen, wenn sie es tut", sagt Ursula.

"Das ist richtig", sagt ihre Mutter. "Und wenn sie fertig ist, bist du auch fertig."

"Was wenn man noch nicht fertig ist?" fragt Ursula.

"Man hört einfach auf", sagt ihre Mutter. "Und du musst warten, bis die Königin sitzt."

"Bevor man sich setzt?" sagt Ursula.

"Richtig", sagt ihre Mutter. Ursula denkt darüber nach. Es gibt viele Regeln, wenn man Königin oder Prinzessin ist. Ursula und ihre Mutter essen zu Ende. Sie gehen schlafen.

www.LearnLikeNatives.com

Am nächsten Morgen wacht Ursula auf. Sie ist nervös wegen des Wettbewerbs. Heute verkünden sie den Sieger. Sie **frühstückt** mit ihrer Mutter.

"Ich bin nervös", sagt sie.

"Ursula, du wirst nicht gewinnen", sagt ihre Mutter. "So viele Leute nehmen am Wettbewerb teil."

"Ach," sagt Ursula. Sie ist traurig. Sie isst ihr **Müsli**. Sie hat keinen Hunger. Sie hat den **Speck** und die **Eier** nicht einmal angerührt.

Sie machen den Fernseher an.

"Und wir verkünden den Gewinner des Wettbewerbs zum Mittagessen mit der Königin", sagt der Mann im Fernsehen. Er steckt seine

www.LearnLikeNatives.com

Hand in eine riesige Glasschale voller Zettel. Er bewegt seine Hand herum. Er zieht ein Zettel heraus. Er öffnet den Zettel.

"Und der Sieger ist ... Ursula Vann!", sagt er.

Ursula sieht ihre Mutter an. Ihre Mutter sieht sie an.

"Hast du das gehört?" fragt sie. Ihre Mutter nickt und starrt sie an. Ihr Mund ist offen.

"Habe ich gewonnen?" fragt sie. Ihre Mutter nickt sprachlos.

"Juhu!" ruft Ursula. "Ich wusste es! Ich werde die Königin kennenlernen!" Ursula beendet ihr Essen und geht zur Schule.

Am nächsten Tag ist der Tag für das Mittagessen mit der Königin. Ursula geht zum Palast. Sie ist verängstigt. Sie ist nur ein junges Mädchen. Das ist ein großes Abenteuer für so ein junges Mädchen.

"Wer bist du?" fragt eine Wache.

"Ursula Vann", sagt sie. "Ich gewann den Wettbewerb, um mit der Königin zu Mittag zu essen."

"Oh, hallo, junge Dame", sagt die Wache. "Du bist ein hübsches junges Mädchen, komm rein."

"Danke", sagt sie.

Eine Wache bringt sie in den Palast. Er ist gewaltig und sehr groß. Sie laufen durch die Hallen. Die

Wache hat einen lustigen Hut. Ursula kichert. Dann hört sie auf. Sie sind im Esszimmer.

Die Königin von England sitzt am Tisch! Vor ihr liegt ein Teller mit **belegten Broten**. Sie ist klein. Sie ist glücklich und sie lächelt.

"Hallo, meine Liebe", sagt sie.

"Guten Tag, Eure Majestät", sagt Ursula. Sie macht einen knicks.

"Danke, dass du zum Mittagessen gekommen bist", sagt sie.

"Es ist mir ein Vergnügen, Eure **Majestät**", sagt Ursula.

"Ich hoffe, es stört dicht nicht. Wir werden Tee anstatt eines förmlichen Mittagessens zu uns nehmen", sagt die Königin. Sie setzt sich wieder. Ursula erinnert sich an ihre Manieren. Sie setzt sich auch.

Die belegten Brote sind königliche belegte Brote, denkt sie. Sie sehen aus wie belegte Brote von zu Hause. Einige haben **Schinken** und **Käse** mit gelbem **Senf**. Andere haben einen **Mayonnaise**salat drauf. Neben einigen **Scones** gibt es einen Teller mit **Keksen**.

"Verzeihung, Eure Majestät", sagt Ursula.

"Ja, meine Liebe", sagt die Königin.

"Was ist auf dem belegten Brot?" fragt sie.

"Oh, das ist mein Lieblingssandwich", sagt die Königin: "Lauch-**Salat**-Sandwich."

"Oh, Lauch", sagt Ursula. Sie fühlt sich krank. Die Königin greift nach einem. Sie nimmt einen Bissen.

"Nimm eins, Liebes", sagt die Königin.

"Danke, Eure Majestät", sagt Ursula. Sie nimmt ein Lauch-Sandwich. Sie kann fühlen, wie sich ihr Magen dreht. Sie nimmt einen riesigen Bissen, weil sie so nervös ist. Ihr Gesicht wird weiß, dann grün.

"Alles in Ordnung, Liebes?" fragt die Königin. "Du siehst nicht gut aus."

"Mir geht es gut", sagt Ursula. Sie fühlt, wie sich ihr Magen dreht. Sie hat das Gefühl, sich übergeben zu müssen. Sie kann den Lauch nicht davon abhalten, wieder ihren Hals hoch zu kommen. Zumindest hielt sie sich an die anderen Regeln für das Mittagessen mit der Königin, denkt sie sich. Niemand hat je etwas von Erbrechen gesagt.

ZUSAMMENFASSUNG

Ursula ist ein junges Mädchen. Sie lebt in London, England. Sie ist besessen von der königlichen Familie. Sie isst mit ihrer Mutter zu Abend und sieht fern. Im Fernsehen verkünden sie einen Wettbewerb. Der Sieger darf mit der Königin zu Mittag essen. Am nächsten Tag, beim Frühstück, verkünden sie den Sieger: Es ist Ursula! Sie geht zum Mittagessen in den Buckingham Palace. Sie folgt den Regeln für das Essen mit der Königin. Die Königin hat spezielle belegte Brote zubereitet. Leider ist Lauchsalat nicht Ursulas Lieblingsessen. Sie fühlt sich krank, als sie sieht, wie die Königin das Sandwich isst.

VOKABELLISTE

ist	is
hat	has
sein	to be
haben	have
sind	are
Lauch	leeks
bin	am
Gemüse	vegetable
Karotten	carrots

www.LearnLikeNatives.com

Brokkoli	broccoli
Salat	salad
Mittag	lunch
muss	have to
Nachtisch	dessert
Trauben	grapes
Kirschen	cherries
Früchte	fruit
Sahne	cream
Zucker	sugar
Essen	meal
frühstückt	breakfast
Müsli	cereal
Eier	eggs
Speck	bacon
belegte Brote	sandwiches

Tee	tea
Schinken	ham
Käse	cheese
Senf	mustard
Kekse	cookies
Scones	scones
Salat	salad

FRAGEN

1) Was passiert, wenn Ursula zum ersten Mal Lauch probiert?

    a) sie liebt ihn

    b) ihre Mutter verbrennt ihn

    c) sie muss sich fast erbrechen

    d) sie merkt es nicht

www.LearnLikeNatives.com

2) Was ist eine Regel, wenn Sie mit der Königin von England essen?

    a) Sie dürfen erst essen, wenn sie isst

    b) Sie müssen blau tragen

    c) Sie müssen Sandwiches essen

    d) Sie müssen sich setzen bevor sie sitzt

3) Was hält Ursulas Mutter von dem Wettbewerb?

    a) Ursula hat eine Chance zu gewinnen

    b) es ist Betrug

    c) die Königin sollte nicht beteiligt sein

    d) Ursula wird niemals gewinnen

4) Was hat die Königin zum Mittagessen?

    a) ein guter Braten

    b) Lachs, ihr Favorit

    c) Teekekse und Sandwiches

d) es ist streng geheim

.

5) Welche der folgenden Aussagen ist wahr?

a) Ursula geht mitten im Essen

b) Ursula kann ihre Reaktion auf Lauch nicht kontrollieren

c) die Königin hat die belegten Brote selbst gemacht

d) Sandwiches sind kein gutes Mittagessen

ANTWORTEN

1) Was passiert, wenn Ursula zum ersten Mal Lauch probiert?

c) sie muss sich fast erbrechen

www.LearnLikeNatives.com

2) Was ist eine Regel, wenn Sie mit der Königin von England essen?

    a) Sie dürfen erst essen, wenn sie isst

3) Was hält Ursulas Mutter von dem Wettbewerb?

    d) Ursula wird niemals gewinnen

4) Was hat die Königin zum Mittagessen?

    c) Teekekse und Sandwiches

5) Welche der folgenden Aussagen ist wahr?

    b) Ursula kann ihre Reaktion auf Lauch nicht kontrollieren

Translation of the Story

Lunch with The Queen

STORY

Ursula **is** a young girl. She lives in London, England. She studies at school. She loves to bake. She **has** an obsession: the royal family. She wants **to be** a princess.

One night, Ursula is at home. Her mother prepares her dinner. They **have** something new. Her mother brings the plate to the table.

"What **are** those?" asks Ursula.

"These are **leeks**," says Ursula's mom.

"Oh, I don't like leeks," says Ursula.

"Try them," says her mom. She tries them. She almost vomits.

"I **am** sick," says Ursula.

"No, you are not," says her mom.

"Please, give me any other **vegetable**," says Ursula. "**Carrots**, **broccoli**, **salad**?"

"Oh, Ursula, just eat your **meat** then," says her mom. She turns on the television. They watch the news. The report is about the Queen of England. Ursula stops eating. She pays close attention.

"Queen Elizabeth reigns in England for 68 years," says the news report. "She is married to Prince Phillip. They have four children."

The news report talks about the Queen. She lives in Buckingham Palace. She is very healthy, despite her age.

"I want to visit Buckingham Palace," says Ursula.

"Yes, dear," says her mom. They watch the program. The program announces a special competition. One person can win a visit to Buckingham Palace. The winner will eat **lunch** with the queen. Ursula screams.

"I **have to** win!" she shouts.

"I don't know," says her mom. "Many people enter the contest."

Ursula watches the program. She learns how to enter. She takes a picture of herself eating. Then she posts it on social media. She watches the program, which talks about eating with the Queen. She watches as they show what happened to a prince from the South Pacific.

The Queen is on a boat with the prince. They serve **dessert**. The prince forgets to watch the Queen. He takes some **grapes** and some **cherries** from the **fruit** on the table and puts them in his bowl. He pours **cream** over them. He sprinkles **sugar** on top. He starts to eat, and then he realizes the Queen has not. He makes a big mistake. The Queen takes her spoon. She eats a bit. That makes the prince feel better. He is very embarrassed.

"There are rules to eat with the Queen?" she asks her mom.

"Of course," says her mom.

"Like what?" asks Ursula.

"Well, the Queen begins the **meal** and ends the meal," says Ursula's mom.

"You mean you can't eat until she does," says Ursula.

"That's right," says her mom. "And when she finishes, you finish, too."

"What if you aren't finished?" asks Ursula.

"You are," says her mom. "And you must wait for the Queen to sit."

"Before you sit?" says Ursula.

"Right," says her mom. Ursula thinks about this. There are lots of rules if you are queen or princess. Ursula and her mom finish dinner. They go to sleep.

The next morning, Ursula wakes up. She is nervous about the contest. Today they announce the winner. She eats **breakfast** with her mom.

"I am nervous," she says.

"Ursula, you won't win," says her mom. "So many people are in the contest."

"Oh," says Ursula. She is sad. She eats her **cereal**. She is not hungry. Her **bacon** and **eggs** sit untouched.

They turn on the television.

"And we announce the winner of the Lunch with the Queen Contest," says the man on the TV. He puts his hand into a huge glass bowl full of papers. He moves his hand around. He pulls out a paper. He opens the paper.

"And the winner is…Ursula Vann!" he says.

Ursula looks at her mom. Her mom looks at her.

"Did you hear that?" she asks. Her mom nods, staring. Her mouth is open.

"Did I win?" she asks. Her mom nods, speechless.

"Woo-hoo!" shouts Ursula. "I knew I would! I'm going to see the queen!" Ursula finishes her food and goes to school.

The next day is the day for lunch with the Queen. Ursula walks up to the palace. She is terrified. She is only a young girl. This is a big adventure for such a young girl.

"Who are you?" asks a guard.

"Ursula Vann," she says. "I won the contest to have lunch with the Queen."

"Oh, hello, young lady," the guard says. "You are a pretty young lass. Come in."

"Thank you," she says.

A guard takes her to the palace. It is grand, and very big. They walk through the halls. The guard has a funny hat. Ursula giggles. Then, she stops. They are in the dining room.

The Queen of England is sitting at the table! There is a plate of **sandwiches** in front of her. She is small. She is happy, and she is smiling.

"Hello, dear," she says.

"Hello, your majesty," Ursula says. She courtsies.

"Thank you for coming to lunch," she says.

"It is my pleasure, your **Majesty**," says Ursula.

"I hope you don't mind. We will be having **tea** instead of a proper lunch," says the Queen. She sits again. Ursula remembers her manners. She sits, too.

The sandwiches are royal sandwiches, she thinks. They look a lot like sandwiches from home, though. Some have **ham** and **cheese**, with a yellow bit of **mustard**. Others have a **mayonnaise** salad on them. There is a plate of **cookies** next to some **scones**.

"Pardon me, your Majesty," says Ursula.

"Yes, dear?" says the Queen.

"What is on that sandwich?" she asks.

"Oh, that's my favorite," says the Queen. "Leek **salad** sandwich."

"Oh, leeks," says Ursula. She feels sick. The Queen reaches for one. She takes a bite.

"Have one, dear," says the Queen.

"Thank you, your Majesty," says Ursula. She takes a leek sandwich. She can feel her stomach turn. She takes a huge bite because she is so nervous. Her face turns white, then green.

"Are you alright, dear?" asks the Queen. "You look quite unwell."

"I- I- I'm fine," says Ursula. She feels her stomach turning. She feels as if she will vomit. She can't stop the leeks from coming back up her throat. At least she followed the other rules for eating lunch with the Queen, she thinks. Nobody ever said anything about vomiting.

www.LearnLikeNatives.com

www.LearnLikeNatives.com

CONCLUSION

You did it!

You finished a whole book in a brand new language. That in and of itself is quite the accomplishment, isn't it?

Congratulate yourself on time well spent and a job well done. Now that you've finished the book, you have familiarized yourself with over 500 new vocabulary words, comprehended the heart of 3 short stories, and listened to loads of dialogue unfold, all without going anywhere!

Charlemagne said "To have another language is to possess a second soul." After immersing yourself in this book, you are broadening your horizons and opening a whole new path for yourself.

Have you thought about how much you know now that you did not know before? You've learned everything from how to greet and how to express your emotions to basics like colors and place words. You can tell time and ask question. All without opening a schoolbook. Instead, you've cruised through fun, interesting stories and possibly listened to them as well.

Perhaps before you weren't able to distinguish meaning when you listened to German. If you used the audiobook, we bet you can now pick out meanings and words when you hear someone speaking. Regardless, we are sure you have taken an important step to being more fluent. You are well on your way!

Best of all, you have made the essential step of distinguishing in your mind the idea that most often hinders people studying a new language. By approaching German through our short stories and dialogs, instead of formal lessons with just grammar and vocabulary, you are no longer in the 'learning' mindset. Your approach is much more similar to an osmosis, focused on speaking and using the language, which is the end goal, after all!

So, what's next?

This is just the first of five books, all packed full of short stories and dialogs, covering essential, everyday German that will ensure you master the basics. You can find the rest of the books in the series, as well as a whole host of other resources, at LearnLikeNatives.com. Simply add the book to your library to take the next step in your language learning journey. If you are ever in need of new ideas or direction, refer to our 'Speak Like a Native' eBook, available to you for free at LearnLikeNatives.com, which clearly outlines practical steps you can take to continue learning any language you choose.

www.LearnLikeNatives.com

We also encourage you to get out into the real world and practice your German. You have a leg up on most beginners, after all—instead of pure textbook learning, you have been absorbing the sound and soul of the language. Do not underestimate the foundation you have built reviewing the chapters of this book. Remember, no one feels 100% confident when they speak with a native speaker in another language.

One of the coolest things about being human is connecting with others. Communicating with someone in their own language is a wonderful gift. Knowing the language turns you into a local and opens up your world. You will see the reward of learning languages for many years to come, so keep that practice up!. Don't let your fears stop you from taking the chance to use your German. Just give it a try, and remember that you will make mistakes. However, these mistakes will teach you so much, so view every single one as a small victory! Learning is growth.

www.LearnLikeNatives.com

Don't let the quest for learning end here! There is so much you can do to continue the learning process in an organic way, like you did with this book. Add another book from Learn Like a Native to your library. Listen to German talk radio. Watch some of the great German Musical. Put on the latest CD from Sarah Connor. Take cooking lessons in German. Whatever you do, don't stop because every little step you take counts towards learning a new language, culture, and way of communicating.

www.LearnLikeNatives.com

www.LearnLikeNatives.com

www.LearnLikeNatives.com

Learn Like a Native is a revolutionary **language education brand** that is taking the linguistic world by storm. Forget boring grammar books that never get you anywhere, Learn Like a Native teaches you languages in a fast and fun way that actually works!

As an international, multichannel, language learning platform, we provide **books, audio guides and eBooks** so that you can acquire the knowledge you need, swiftly and easily.

Our **subject-based learning**, structured around real-world scenarios, builds your conversational muscle and ensures you learn the content most relevant to your requirements.
Discover our tools at ***LearnLikeNatives.com***.

When it comes to learning languages, we've got you covered!

www.ingramcontent.com/pod-product-compliance
Lightning Source LLC
Chambersburg PA
CBHW070042230426
43661CB00005B/724